COMMUNICATING WITH **CONFIDENCE**™

PROFESSIONAL CONNECTIONS

LEARNING HOW TO NETWORK

SUZANNE WEINICK

New York

Published in 2012 by The Rosen Publishing Group, Inc.
29 East 21st Street, New York, NY 10010

Library of Congress Cataloging-in-Publication Data

Weinick, Suzanne.
Professional connections: learning how to network/Suzanne Weinick.—1st ed.
    p. cm.—(Communicating with confidence)
Includes bibliographical references and index.
ISBN 978-1-4488-5520-9 (library binding)—
ISBN 978-1-4488-5635-0 (pbk.)—
ISBN 978-1-4488-5636-7 (6-pack)
1. Business networks—Juvenile literature.
2. Business communication—Juvenile literature. I. Title.
HD69.S8W44 2012
650.1'3—dc22

                                              2011013698

Manufactured in the United States of America

CPSIA Compliance Information: Batch #W12YA: For further information, contact Rosen Publishing, New York, New York, at 1-800-237-9932.

CONTENTS

INTRODUCTION

Many of us have heard the phrase, "It is not what you know, but who you know." The meaning behind this statement is that networking is a key component in putting yourself in the right place to achieve success. Networking is applying your interpersonal skills in a professional setting to meet new people and make new connections. Every person that you know may someday be a potential client, employer, or coworker. The key is to learn how to make your relationships work to your advantage and to capitalize on your network of contacts. An important element of networking is to make sure that your connections with people are not only online, through Web-based communities, but also through face-to-face relationships. You must be able to have conversations with individuals on a personal level in order to enhance your communication skills. This will be vital to building a career and establishing life-long mentor relationships.

Social networking Web sites function as online communities that connect people with common interests, political or religious beliefs, shared backgrounds, and careers. These Web-based communities have flooded the Internet. The most successful of these

Mentors can serve as your professional connections. They can also teach you how to present yourself publicly and give you skills to become an effective leader in your community or professional field of interest.

online social networking sites is Facebook. Facebook has transformed the way people distribute information about themselves and receive information about their friends. The identity you create on Facebook is your global résumé.

In the age of Facebook and other social sites like LinkedIn and Twitter, social networking is a very public forum for building connections. Many experts believe that the intimacy of personal conversations is becoming a lost art. However, to get noticed in this vast network of people, you must be able to navigate cyberspace and have personal interaction skills. People who create their own profile or page on these online networking sites must learn to manage and display this information. As with any new skill, learning to network effectively takes practice and planning.

Networking is creating personal relationships that are helpful to both parties. As the Internet continues to evolve with new ways to connect users all over the world, networking will continue to change to use the new technology. The key is to keep your contact information organized so that your network can propel you to succeed in your professional life. Networking is an important skill for job searching and career building.

FINDING YOUR CONTACTS

There is a big difference between casual conversation and connecting to another individual. Yet, even if your goal in speaking to someone is to ultimately get a job, you need to make a personal connection. When you meet someone for the first time, you need to find common interests or experiences to convert a stranger into a friend or professional colleague. The technique for making this transformation is the art of social interaction. There is no formula to create a personal connection, but there are skills to learn in order to make the process work for you.

Networking is building connections on a personal level. It is difficult to approach a

Attending seminars and conferences is a great way to practice your face-to-face networking skills. It's also an excellent way to meet new people to add to your circle of contacts.

stranger in a room full of people. The first step is to be your-self and allow others to see the real you. When you approach someone, you should have a genuine desire to learn something about that person. You need to ask questions that prompt the other person to share information about himself or herself: "How long have you been in New York?" "Where did you go to school?" These are the types of questions that create a personal conversation and can give you information about the person's life, values, and interests. These are all ways to form a personal connection with a new acquaintance.

Once someone shares information with you, you can share similar information with him or her about yourself. You may find that someone has shared interests with you, and that can lead to a meaningful connection. It is helpful to let someone know that you are involved in groups or organizations pertaining to your mutual interests. Even mentioning that you have read a good book or article about a shared interest could lead to a stronger personal connection.

Face-to-face interaction with others can be awkward for some people, especially if it is a new type of communication with strangers. It is critical to connect with people who will help you reach your goals on a personal and professional level. These people are the ones who will provide you with feedback and advice; they are role models and mentors.

Making Body Language Work for You

Body language is a nonverbal form of communication that all of us use and interpret every day. It is made up of facial

Making a good first impression by presenting yourself in a professional manner is key to positive body language.

expressions, body posture, tone of voice, hand gestures, and eye movements that result in subconscious interpretation of a person's thoughts. Body language creates a social perception and can have an impact on the meaning of verbal communication. Janine Driver, the author of *You Say More Than You Think* and the founder and president of the Body Language Institute, located in Washington, D.C., says that every person has a natural ability to be successful at body language. "We just need to learn to tap into it." According to Driver, "Over 50 percent of what we communicate with others is nonverbal." Therefore, learning to use your body language can improve your ability to be confident in social situations.

For example, the handshake is a powerful first impression gesture. This initial contact with someone says, "Let's connect." A business handshake should be no more than three seconds. The handshake should be firm but not bone-crushing. Smile, maintain eye contact, and listen in order to use body language to your advantage.

First impressions are critical when trying to establish a new network contact. Your outside appearance should match the image you want to portray. It is important not to distract from your first impression with clothing, body art, or accessories that send the wrong message.

Understanding body language cues will allow you to make an accurate assessment of a person's intentions. Awareness of your own body language when communicating with others will make you appear confident and secure. This will help you learn to always be your best self and will lead to success.

School is your first opportunity to work on becoming a good communicator. You should speak clearly, listen carefully, and make eye contact with your teacher.

Paying Attention

When you are listening to someone give you information, you need to give your visual and mental attention to the person speaking. This means focusing on what he or she is saying and processing the information so that you can recall it later. Eye contact is important in connecting with what the speaker is saying. Don't be distracted by background conversations or movements. This will help you stay focused and assist your brain in recalling information received.

The information you gather from a new acquaintance may be valuable to you in the future. The more you remember about the other person, the better you will fare when

Six Degrees of Separation

In the late 1960s, social psychologist Stanley Milgram conducted research on the shortest path between two complete strangers (5.5 links). Milgram's theory was the inspiration for the play *Six Degrees of Separation* by John Guare (which was also made into a movie). By 1995, the idea that we are all somehow connected to each other became known as the six degrees of separation theory. A game that connects people to actor Kevin Bacon was even created.

Columbia University professor Duncan Watts has studied network theory, the scientific field that examines how networks form and how they work in society. Professor Watts created Columbia's Small World Project, which is an online experiment that assigns each "participant" a random "target" (one of eighteen people around the world) to see how many e-mails it takes to get from someone the participant already knows to the target person. According to *ABC News* reporter Thomas Berman, approximately sixty thousand people from more than 170 countries participated in the Small World Project as of December 2006, and the average number of links in the human chains was six. Therefore, the theory of six degrees of separation was proved with the use of the Internet. Naturally, the Internet has been a perfect medium to prove the hypothesis that we are all closely connected if we just connect the links between us. Facebook has been a catalyst in showing how close the relationships are to each other and how you can use this interconnectedness to network on a professional level.

you meet up again or come in contact with that person through social networking sites. If you remember where the person grew up, what pets she had, or something interesting about her family, it will show that you were listening when she spoke to you initially.

Self-Assessment

Your personal goals and values influence the choices you make when deciding who to "friend" on Facebook, the chat rooms you visit online, and the blogs that interest you. However, most successful people will tell you that they became who they are because of the people they interacted with throughout their lives. This includes, high school and college counselors, teachers and mentors, coaches, employers, and leaders of volunteer organizations. These are people who help others reach their short-term and long-term goals. These people are also a great resource for you to find a job that will utilize your specific skills and training.

Enhancing your personal networking skills is critical to becoming a mature adult. Having the ability to make connections with others will prepare you for the challenges of job interviews, interacting with coworkers, and obtaining a leadership position in the future. The goal is to build meaningful relationships without sacrificing your integrity or using other people only to attain your own objectives. If you have special interests or hobbies, you can find others who share those interests by joining a club or searching for online groups.

CHAPTER 2

BUILDING YOUR PROFESSIONAL NETWORK

t is difficult to get a job coming straight out of school with little or no experience. It is especially tough if you do not have professional connections in your chosen field. Those who succeed in landing a job are those individuals who have invested the necessary time and effort into creating relationships that can help them prior to the commencement of their job search. This means that you can start making professional connections while you are in high school, college, or graduate school. Every person you know is a contact who can help you find a job or further your career.

If you are interested in a career that has workplace training via an apprenticeship or internship, you will learn new job skills and the ability to work with professionals.

At some point during high school or college, you will likely determine what you will do to make a living as an adult. This can be a very overwhelming challenge, but it can also be a time of personal growth. The best way to decide what path to take with respect to a career is to investigate areas that interest you. Knowing your strengths and weaknesses is critical to creating a successful plan of action. If you think that you may be interested in a certain career, it is a good idea to work in that field, even if it is as a volunteer, through an unpaid internship, or at an entry-level position during the weekends or summer vacation. This will afford you the opportunity to be around other people who work in that field. It will also provide you with the information about what technical skills and educational requirements are needed to be successful in your chosen career.

Making professional connections even at a young age will get you in the habit of looking at every new relationship as one that can enrich your life and your career path. You should approach others in a work environment with confidence and enthusiasm. It is critical to be on time and give your full attention when going for an interview or attending a meeting or training session.

An important part of creating successful networking relationships is speaking in a strong voice with body language that reflects self-confidence. There are many subtle forms of body language that affect people's perceptions of each other. These include eye movements, hand gestures, facial expressions, and posture.

Be Confident

Perfecting your networking skills will help you become your own best advocate. Tonya Reiman, author of *The Yes Factor: Get What You Want. Say What You Mean. The Power of Persuasive Communication*, tells her readers to break out of their comfort zone to approach a new contact and make a meaningful connection. For example, refusing to give into shyness and initiating a conversation will be difficult and uncomfortable at first. However, with practice, learning to start a conversation will lead to personal growth.

Business Cards

Business cards usually have only basic contact information on them: name, title, phone number, e-mail, and office address. Tommy Spaulding, founder and president of a leadership-development consulting firm, suggests that you write on the back of someone's business card information you obtain after talking to that person. For example, you may find out through a conversation with a company president that he loves to ski, is an avid photographer, and has two teenagers who enjoy tennis. By obtaining this information, you can move to a higher level in your relationship with that person.

Even though you may not get a business card from every new person you meet, it is important to get to know people on a personal level. You may find that the activities they participate in and the organizations they are involved in are things that you have an interest in, too. These connections will give you a unique chance to reach out to that person in a personal way.

To gain confidence in new social networking situations, you should be able to speak confidently about yourself. Make a list of your positive traits and be prepared to describe your educational background, your work experiences, and your unique skills. Present an image of yourself that reflects the skills you have that can make you successful in your career choices.

Know Your Audience

Whether you are on a job interview, at a business convention, or attending a career seminar, you will be more relaxed if you are prepared before you go. This requires that you gain knowledge of the company you are visiting or learn about the industry you are networking within. This is called doing your professional homework by acquiring insight about current issues affecting a business or industry. The more well-read you are on various news events and topics of interest, the easier it will be for you to make an informed statement if there is a pause in a conversation you are engaged in. The objective is to be prepared, and this will bolster your confidence.

Do not be controversial when choosing a topic to discuss with new acquaintances. Demonstrate self-control when it comes to expressing opinions in a professional conversation. Ask questions that are appropriate to the setting and show that you have knowledge about the industry or business ideas being discussed. Being genuinely interested in what someone has to say will go a long way in keeping a conversation going.

"Joining in" by attending meetings and participating in events that arouse your interests can help you discover your career path.

Solicit Feedback

Another important component of social networking is soliciting feedback from a colleague or mentor. It can be an informal assessment of whether that person believes that you have made contributions to a business meeting or discussion. Talk to your supervisor after you have completed a new task at your job or internship and ask her to review your performance. Consider every new experience as a chance to grow and learn about how to improve your skills and abilities. Feedback will help you evaluate your competence at making your mark on new contacts. You need to be open to criticism. Positive feedback can be turned into a reference for future jobs and opportunities. Constructive feedback will give you a chance to improve your skills to achieve your future goals.

Networking Resources

While you are in high school and college, take advantage of part-time jobs, volunteer opportunities, and internships. These opportunities expose you to new networking contacts. They also give you a chance to explore different vocational choices that may

Volunteering your time and talents in your community will help others, and it can lead to new relationships that will enhance your professional connections.

work for you. People from all walks of life and varied experiences routinely participate in community service. Volunteering provides the ability to use leadership and organizational skills to make a difference in your community. By involving yourself in different types of activities, you open yourself up to working with people from different backgrounds, religions, and heritages. This will enlighten

Beware of Multitasking

Most people think that they can do multiple things at the same time; this is known as multitasking. However, when you multitask, you interfere with the brain's ability to store information in short-term memory. The average person receives hundreds of messages every day via e-mail, text messages, and television and radio advertisements. This enormous volume of information clouds our minds and makes it hard for us to concentrate on what is important. You should unplug and turn off personal electronic devices when you need to focus on one activity or project. Multitasking can also be costly and dangerous—do not send text messages while driving or operating equipment.

Maggie Jackson, author of *Distracted: The Erosion of Attention and the Coming Dark Age*, says multitasking causes "stress and frustration and lowered creativity" because the interruption causes the brain to have attention fragmentation. You should realize that not all communication is effective if it is written without thought and review. Distracted texting, e-mailing, and blogging makes your words meaningless. Jackson points out that multitasking makes us "less and less able to see, hear, and comprehend what's relevant and permanent." Once distracted, it takes approximately twenty-five minutes to return to the interrupted task. This is very unproductive and has a negative impact on critical thinking skills.

you about the common things that connect people. Local clubs, religious groups, and volunteer organizations are always looking for new participants to donate time and effort.

Internships

Internships are a great way to explore career interests and get work experience in a chosen field. Most of these opportunities are available for high school or college students. They are usually volunteer or low-paid, short-term positions that could lead to future employment opportunities. Internships are an

Building your résumé by embracing new opportunities will open doors for you in the future. A broad range of skills learned through school, work, and clubs will make you more marketable as an employee.

important way to make contacts in industries of interest to you and to build your résumé. In order to get an internship, you may have to complete an application. But some internships are created when someone inquires about a position in a business that could use part-time help from someone willing to learn.

Many people, when asked how they ended up in their job or industry, will respond that there were a series of fortunate events that led them to where they are today. These fortunate events are not coincidences because these same people were very good at networking with their peers, mentors, and colleagues. Unexpected professional opportunities can also arise out of community service activities and volunteer work.

Your Work Environment

Whether it is an entry-level position or a job that you have worked at for a long time, you should be aware of what is happening in the organization. Every office or work environment has an institutional culture. You will need to communicate with your coworkers and superiors to determine the way things are done in the office, factory, or store. Ask questions before you make a mistake—do not be overconfident. If you are not sure how the company you are working for does something, find out from someone who knows. For example, you should know what the procedures are for taking a day off. Do you need to get written approval from a superior? Some organizations or work environments are highly structured and others are more flexible. It is critical to exhibit a strong work ethic. This means you get to meetings on time, you learn the names of colleagues, and you refrain from taking the easy way out when a task is presented.

Make people aware of your presence. When attending conventions, trade shows, and meetings, your goal should be to make new contacts and pay attention to name tags. Sometimes you will find an immediate connection to people, and sometimes you will have to work at finding a common interest.

MYTHS
and
facts

Myth: Introverted, or shy, people can never be good networkers.

Fact: Introverts can be just as good at networking as outgoing people. Introverts are usually people who need to be confident before they speak about something. This means if you do your research before you approach new people, you will gain the self-confidence to enter new relationships and form lasting network connections. Practice speaking out loud to your friends and you will gain the ability to speak publicly with strangers. Many schools offer courses in public speaking that are valuable no matter what career path you choose.

Myth: Networking online is the same as face-to-face interaction.

Fact: Face-to-face interaction allows individuals to connect on a deeper level than online through social networking sites. You can read someone's body language, change topics rapidly, and connect with someone in a more personal manner. In addition, people remember faces differently than they remember words and names. If you want to stand out from the crowd, you need to make an impression on someone by meeting him or her in person.

Myth: You can say whatever you want online because it is a medium of true expression.

Fact: The Internet is an open public forum. If you say negative things about a difficult high school teacher, those words may come back to haunt you when they are discovered by a potential employer or a college scholarship committee. For all its positive attributes, providing free access to information sharing around the world, it is also a place where words and images never go away. Be aware that there is always a trail that leads back to you.

CONNECTING ONLINE

Most high school students will meet their college roommates online before they meet them in person at an orientation. High school and college students today experience campus life in both the real and virtual world. Students all over the world can share information about clubs, social action causes, political activism, and events on campus through social networks online and on mobile devices. Each time a student joins an online group, posts a comment or picture, or participates in an online conversation, that student has to decide if his or her response or participation will be appropriate and ethical. These

Mark Zuckerberg is the founder of Facebook. *Time* magazine named him 2010 Person of the Year. On his own Facebook page, he takes credit for "making the world more open and connected" for hundreds of millions of people.

are very difficult decisions to make, but your online reputation is on the line.

Employers and employment search companies are beginning to use social networking sites like Facebook and LinkedIn to search for potential candidates that have specific educational backgrounds, past experience in certain fields, and a geographic location convenient for job placements. Therefore, it is critical that your profile on a social networking site accurately reflects your job experience, educational degrees, and expertise in your field. Equally important is to keep your personal life private.

Facebook

Facebook is probably the first social networking site most people will become familiar with between the ages of sixteen and twenty-one. Facebook started as a personal network to help college students stay in touch with friends. It has now expanded its scope to include connecting people based on prior business contacts that could lead to finding a job or connecting with a professional community.

Learning to use Facebook to your advantage is a great way to build solid social networks with people who will enhance your life. Posting messages on your "wall" will prompt your "friends" to interact with you. Reading other people's messages many lead you to new contacts and provide leads for educational or business opportunities. If someone is looking for help and you give him or her assistance, you will find that those you collaborate with will give you guidance when you ask for it.

About Facebook and Twitter

Facebook is a privately held company founded in 2004 by Mark Zuckerberg. It was created as a way for students at Harvard University to communicate with each other. In 2006, Facebook was made available to the public. On Facebook, you create a profile with information about yourself where friends, family, classmates, and acquaintances can find you. Once people add you as their "friend," you have access to their lives as they exist on their Facebook "wall."

Facebook has been plagued with complaints about privacy issues. It created a new set of privacy controls in 2009. However, users complained that figuring out the privacy settings is too complicated. Zuckerberg has been criticized for being insensitive about third-party access to information shared on Facebook. Ironically, on January 31, 2011, Zuckerberg obtained a restraining order against a man who was harassing him. Despite its problems, Facebook has revolutionized the way people socialize.

Twitter was started in San Francisco, California, in 2006 by a podcasting company. Jack Dorsey, Twitter creator, cofounder, and chairman, was determined to blend e-mail and instant messaging to create "status information" in a Web-based format. Twitter is a short-messaging service inspired by text messages on cell phones. Twitter allows users to send "tweets," which are messages no longer than 140 characters, on its Web site to anyone who wants to "follow" them. Twitter is free, but you must register in order to post messages. Twitter connects strangers with common interests.

Twitter has become a marketing tool for businesses, celebrities, and political activists. However, Twitter is not seen as an effective means of social networking, since it has such a limited message capacity. According to the *New York Times*, Twitter creates real-time commentary on daily activities. In 2009, people in Iran and Moldova organized government protests through Twitter. The 2011 uprising in Egypt is also credited to the use of Twitter and Facebook. In February 2010, Twitter users were sending fifty million tweets per day.

Facebook is a less formal social networking Web site for personal interaction between people who already know each other. If you are constantly going online to solicit a job or advice regarding a personal matter, you may find that others will "de-friend" or "ignore" you. Facebook is about continued positive interaction between "friends." The key component of social networking on Facebook is to be genuine.

Just keep in mind that Facebook is a very public social networking site, and privacy settings are not airtight. Your boss may be able to view your photos, posts, and list of friends, even if you have not become friends with your superior.

LinkedIn

LinkedIn is a professional online networking site. It has become a popular venue for recruiters to find candidates for job opportunities and for people to connect with peers in their careers. Therefore, it is imperative that your online profile highlight your education, job experience, and skills. According to Mark Schnurman, a career coach, your professional profile should use keywords that hiring managers and recruiters use to find candidates. Look at profiles of other people in your career field to see what keywords are used in

LinkedIn (http://www.linkedin.com) is a professional online networking Web site that allows users to create a custom profile to highlight their background, education, current and previous positions, and achievements.

your industry or profession. Schnurman says that you should get recommendations from close contacts to add credibility to your profile. LinkedIn allows users to join up to fifty groups within the site. Many job postings are listed within groups.

LinkedIn is a good online platform for sharing ideas and connecting with industry peers and associates. Many business leaders are on LinkedIn, and you can have access to their years of training and expertise. Creating these professional connections before you need them is a smart move.

Regardless of which personal and professional social networking sites you choose to join, your online profiles should be consistent. There is database crossover between your contacts on personal social networking sites and professional networking sites. Facebook and LinkedIn are the largest and most popular online social networks, but there are many others that are useful. Based on your career, you can find communities through professional organizations and career-oriented sites.

Twitter

Twitter is currently the fastest-growing social networking site in the United States. It is a unique social networking platform that provides real-time short messages. These messages are no longer than 140 characters and are called tweets. Twitter is a microblogging format that allows a person to "follow" a person, organization, group, or business. Twitter is still a fairly new phenomenon, and the site will probably undergo changes as it evolves with the needs and desires of users. It can be used as an efficient way to send microposts to a group of subscribers

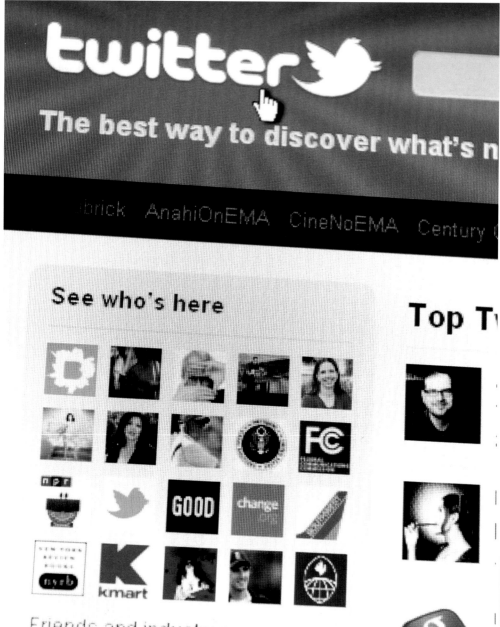

According to its Web site, Twitter (http://www.twitter.com) is an information network made up of 140-character messages called tweets. The user chooses to follow individuals, businesses, or groups that provide "absorbing real-time information that matters to you."

or publicly on the Web site. The social networking component of tweets is that they allow you to express your opinion or your knowledge on a topic or product. The benefit is that if you share your knowledge with others, they will share their knowledge with you. This type of communication could potentially enhance your networking circle, if used correctly.

Many people use Twitter to chat about their weekend plans, fashion picks, celebrity sightings, and friendship drama. If this is what you are tweeting about, you should not include professional contacts in your subscriber list. Use another form of social media, like LinkedIn, to keep business acquaintances informed about your status and appropriate information about you. Companies are starting to post job openings on Twitter, and talented people are being offered opportunities based on interesting tweets.

Keep in Touch

In order to expand your personal network, you need to keep in touch with people you knew from high school and college—including teachers, coaches, and advisers. Traditional methods of communication, such as letter writing and telephone calls, are becoming obsolete. Obviously, Facebook and school-based social networks will help facilitate these connections. The key is not to bombard your contacts will too many messages. General updates about your current employment status and what you are working on may be enough to keep people informed but not overburdened by your status. Networking for your future is a constant job that takes effort.

As technology continues to evolve, devices such as smartphones and other wireless equipment like tablet computers will flood the market. This will make it easier to stay connected with your social network such as Facebook (http://www.facebook.com) at all times.

There is proper protocol with respect to online communications. You should treat people with respect and remember that networking is a two-way street. The benefit of all online social networks is that they provide you with constant access to a global community. Facebook, LinkedIn, and Twitter can be used on a computer, cell phone, or tablet computer. This means that you can always be connected with your family, friends, colleagues, and contacts. However, you should always be aware of the content, style, and tone of your messages.

Professional networking sites allow you to create an online résumé with your education and work experience, but what does not come out is your unique personality. Only in-person meetings will allow you to present yourself fully. Therefore, connecting online might be a start to a relationship, but it will not reach its full potential until you meet face-to-face. Online social networking sites will continue to grow and change as users interact with each other. Privacy and profile management will be major issues that will affect which social networking sites will survive in this competitive field.

10 Great Questions
TO ASK A GUIDANCE COUNSELOR

1. How can I begin looking for places where I can make professional connections?

2. What are the benefits of an internship, and where can I find one?

3. I'm afraid of public speaking, though I know it's important for my career. How can I get over my fear?

4. How can getting involved in my community help me make professional connections?

5. How can I safely use social networking sites to promote myself?

6. What are the best sites to use to create a profile showing my skills and experiences?

7. How do I post my information on the Internet without risking identity theft?

8. How should I dress for a professional interview?

9. How should I organize my personal and business contacts?

10. What body language should I use to show a speaker that I am listening?

ONLINE ETIQUETTE AND SAFETY

S
ocial networking is the process of using Web-based tools to connect with people. Social networking is an online way to stay connected with friends and family, but it can also be used to reach your career and business goals and help others reach their goals as well. Career coaches Ellen Sautter and Dianne Crompton wrote *Find a Job Through Social Networking* as a guide to understanding social networking as an "effective career management" tool in our global marketplace. According to Crompton and Sautter, the benefits of using the Internet for personal and professional gain are enormous, with all of the

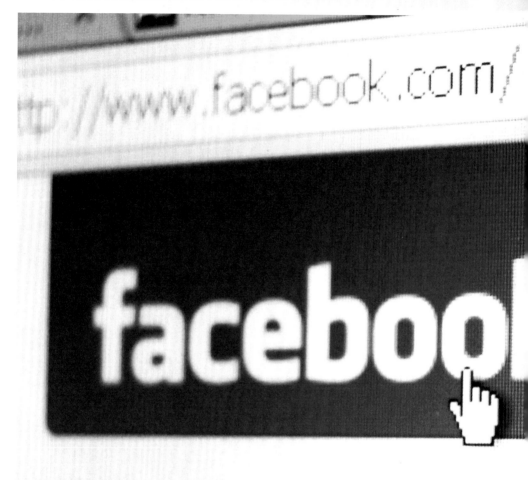

People are spending more and more time on Facebook, Twitter, and other social networking sites. If you find yourself ignoring family and work obligations to network, you may have a compulsion.

discussion groups, blogs, social networking sites, and message boards that are available. However, the problem is that social networking online can also be a huge time-consuming activity with pitfalls that every user should be aware of.

Social networking Web sites function as an online community. These Web-based communities connect people with shared interests, hobbies, political views, careers, and ideas. The big advantage of online networking over face-to-face networking is that you have unlimited access to millions of contacts. The big disadvantage to social networking on the Web is that you need to build trust in your online relationships in a different way. Your online identity must be created carefully and protected at all times. It is important to control how people get your contact information online. Most social networking sites allow users to determine their privacy settings.

Employers, recruiters, and colleges are using social networks and search engines like Google to do "unofficial" background checks on potential employees and high school students applying for admission. Therefore, it is important to remember that everything you say or post online leaves a digital trail that can positively or negatively impact your reputation and character. Crompton and Sautter warn job seekers not to "vent their frustrations" or put personal or social activities online that could detract from their professional brand. Remember that social networking is a way to market yourself to a broader community of potential employers, clients, and business contacts.

Think Before You Write

Writing is one of the fundamental communication skills. Unlike reading, listening, and talking, writing is difficult for many people. There are clear advantages to written communication over the other forms of communication because you have the opportunity to review and revise the written word before you share it or send it to others. Make sure your message is consistent, logical, and clear.

When you are building your social network, you should write to new contacts in a direct and concise manner. Always check your spelling and grammar so that your message is the thing that stands out to the recipient, not your lack of writing skills. If you want to be taken seriously, you need to be adept at composing a well-written e-mail or letter. Thank-you notes or e-mails should be sent to contacts that assist you in achieving your professional goals.

Organize Your E-mail

If you have made important networking contacts that you exchange e-mails with, you need to organize your e-mails in folders. If you leave e-mails in your in-box, you may forget to respond to them or you may accidentally delete them. Always respond promptly to e-mails, even if your response is that you don't have the answer to a question yet but you received the request. In addition, do not bombard a new contact with numerous e-mails. Keep your communications simple and short.

Before you send an electronic response to a potential employer or job recruiter, be sure to read and edit your writing so that it accurately reflects the information you are trying to convey.

Also, you should set up different e-mail addresses for different purposes. One e-mail should be for personal correspondences, and another should be for job searches and professional contacts. This will keep your in-box organized and your business and personal correspondence separate.

Technology Pitfalls

The Internet, cell phones, and e-mail are technologies that have become part of our daily lives. They provide us with constant and immediate information at our fingertips. However, technology can affect our ability to concentrate on schoolwork or tasks that have a deadline. Many people talk about multitasking, which is a way to do multiple things at the same time. The danger with multitasking is that you can easily get distracted by an Internet search, an e-mail exchange, or cell phone calls. Using these technologies too much can cause a lack of focus and a reduced depth of concentration. If your use of technology begins to interfere with the degree of accuracy in your academic or work achievements, you need to cut back on using these devices.

We all want to stay connected with friends, the news, and our personal interests, but using technology to an extreme may become an obsession. According to a Stanford University study, the more one multitasks, the more difficult it becomes to filter out irrelevant information. This could result in poor grades in school or loss of a job. Constantly checking e-mail or Facebook can rise to the level of a technology addiction, and this could negatively affect your productivity. Staying connected at the appropriate time and place is a good thing to do, but refrain from using technology to a fault.

You may want to create another e-mail address for signing up for online newsletters, shopping sites, and general correspondences with businesses that you do not have an individual contact for. Then you can more effectively view your e-mails and filter out those that you do not want to continue to receive, without compromising your entire e-mail account.

Web Searches

Searching the Web is an amazing resource for information and networking. The problem is that anyone can post, comment,

Today, everyone seems to be posting videos, creating blogs, and publishing information on the Internet on sites like YouTube (http://www.youtube.com). Always check multiple sources to confirm the accuracy of facts you obtain from Web-based information.

blog, and write on the Internet, and it is difficult to determine the expertise or knowledge of those "experts" online. Therefore, you must be cautious when relying on information found on the Internet. YouTube is another social media site that engages people through video posts. The important thing to note is that any content posted on the Web should be viewed with skepticism based on the source of the information. You should filter out content that is posted by groups and organizations that are trying to persuade you to buy, vote on, or think differently about a topic or product.

Google is the leading search engine on the Internet. Performing a Google search can lead to a variety of sources of information. This includes newspapers, magazines, trade publications, university information, and more. Keeping up with the latest news about an industry will help you break into that industry in the future.

Let's Chat

Many people find worthwhile information in chat rooms and message boards online. Chat rooms are places where people meet online in real time to talk about a topic. Chat rooms and message boards are usually organized by special interests or general subject matters. Message boards provide users with the ability to read previous conversations (called threads) on a particular topic or question. You can access chat rooms and message boards through Internet services like AOL and MSN, or by visiting a Web site for a subject, hobby, or interest

Cultivating online relationships through chat rooms is another great way to network. Many chat rooms attract members with common interests and talents.

that you are looking to obtain more information about. These forums allow people to form an interactive community that is the essence of social networking.

People who share your interest in a hobby or recreational activity will probably be people who share your idea of the perfect job or career. You should cultivate relationships with individuals who have common interests. These contacts could be a great resource for future job searches. You can build a connection of mutual trust and reliability that could lead to other ways of connecting on a professional and personal level.

Your online communications should be direct and relevant. Many people read messages on their personal electronic devices and don't have time for lengthy explanations. Make your e-mails, posts, and messages useful and productive. Depending on your goal, you may want to ask questions that elicit a response from the reader.

Most important, never reveal your personal information on a message board or in a chat room. Despite how professional a Web community may appear to be, there are people who might pose as professionals to do you harm. With this in mind, never agree to meet with someone you just connected with online without your guardian's knowledge.

Beware of Online Dangers

The rapid nature of e-mails, texts, and instant messages makes it tempting to be constantly in touch with friends, family, and coworkers. Information overload can lead to making bad choices and costly mistakes. Being addicted to incoming messages makes it difficult for many people to live in the moment and focus on the task at hand. Just because someone sends you a message does not mean that you need to respond instantly. Sometimes it is important to digest information in order to provide an accurate and thoughtful response.

Experts suggest that if you have difficulty processing excessive information, you should turn off your phone or computer messaging feature while you are concentrating on something that needs your full attention. Posts on Facebook and Twitter tweets will be there after completing an assignment or project requiring your concentration. The rule is to take advantage of technology but not to let it rule your life.

If you are the messenger, in the interest of efficiency and time, you need to keep your online communications meaningful and concise. You can embrace the new technologies associated with social networking without becoming overwhelmed by it. Do not let yourself get swallowed up in the nonstop stream of information online.

The Internet is an excellent source of information. But when online, you need to be careful with your personal information. There is the growing problem of online predators and individuals who create fictitious identities. You should be very careful about the amount of personal information you put online. Remember that the Internet is uncensored, and not everyone is who they say they are online.

Images and words shared on Facebook and other social networking sites can migrate out of their "access-restricted networks" and could be indexed by search engines for all the world to see. So be careful what you post online.

Online identity theft is a huge concern. You must beware of scams and spam on the Web that could cause you to give your personal information to strangers. Legitimate Web sites usually require you to log on to connect. You should not share your passwords with anyone. Use common sense and don't open e-mail attachments that you are not expecting.

Online social networking is not a substitute for connecting with people in person. There are dangers in developing relationships with people you know only online. After you have engaged in dialogue with new contacts online, you should work on building a significant level of trust before you meet someone in person. Online communities have evolved to provide forums for those with common interests and ideas. It is smart to make your initial in-person connection with someone you met online in a public location, such as a convention, club meeting, or large public gathering. This will afford you the opportunity to work on your face-to-face interpersonal skills while keeping you safe.

Cyberbullying is becoming a problem on social networking sites. *Wired* magazine reported that minors are most at risk of encountering inappropriate content and encounters online when communicating with other minors. If you experience cyberbullying, inform the social networking site manager and tell an adult you trust. Avoid environments that make you more susceptible to risks, stay on reputable Web sites, and communicate only with people you know or have been referred to by someone you respect.

Your Information for Sale

Facebook and other social networking sites realize that the information you provide online is valuable to advertisers and marketing firms. Therefore, much of your profile information is public, including the music you like, your shopping preferences, and your employment information. All the things that you say you "like" on Facebook become public information. To

Cyberbullying

On September 22, 2010, Rutgers University student Tyler Clementi committed suicide after his roommate and another friend used a Webcam to spy on him. Not only was the use of the Webcam an invasion of privacy, but the roommate used his Twitter account to describe what he viewed on his friend's laptop computer. Three young teenage lives have been destroyed by this incident. Clementi took his own life a few days after his personal encounter was broadcast over the Internet. Even if Clementi's roommate thought his actions were just a college prank, the consequences were irreversible. Clementi's roommate and his friend, who allowed her computer to be used, have withdrawn from college, have been arraigned, and are facing possible criminal charges.

This tragic story is not an isolated incident. Cyberbulling is a growing problem in our society, and we all need to think before we knowingly or accidentally cause emotional distress to others online. Everyone has a right to privacy, and the Internet should not be used for malicious acts or vicious words.

make your profile more private, you have to opt out of certain Facebook applications; it is very complex to figure all of this out. The only way to truly protect your privacy on Facebook is to limit how you use it. It is a good idea to use Facebook only to connect with actual friends, family, and colleagues. Use your Web browser to conduct searches for products, information, and music.

You are responsible for what you post online. Facebook posting can have serious legal consequences. Law enforcement will prosecute for inappropriate postings online. Students have been suspended from school or prosecuted for underage drinking or using drugs because of pictures posted on Facebook.

In January 2010, *USA Today* reported that a seventeen-year-old Tennessee high school basketball star was expelled from school for threats posted on Facebook. In another incident, a teacher in Georgia was forced to resign after a parent complained after viewing the teacher's Facebook page and seeing the teacher drinking alcohol while on vacation. It is becoming more common for schools to discipline students and staff for behavior conducted online. In general, there is limited privacy on social networking sites.

CHAPTER 5

NETWORKING TO SUCCESS

In a *Times Union* article, "The 8 Keys to Networking," Tom Denham discusses the do's and don'ts of networking. He calls networking the number-one job search strategy. Denham points out that although people feel awkward and nervous about reaching out to a potential contact, most people enjoy talking about their jobs and are willing to give realistic, and free, advice. Therefore, it is essential to practice the art of networking because it will pay off in the long run.

It is critical to make time to expand and enhance your network circle. This will require you to be organized and to prepare for meeting people in your career. Many experts suggest that you keep a network log of new contacts and information about them. You should schedule brief meetings with people in your network on a regular basis and not only when you need a job. Another important element in building a strategic network is to be a good listener. Ask questions about what your contact person does in his or her job and how the person has moved up successfully within the company. Listening to the answers to these questions may provide you with information on how to handle your own career opportunities.

Good Listening

Listening is the key to successful communication. When you show people that you are concentrating on what they are saying, you make them feel validated and valued. Psychologist Michael P. Nichols says in *The Lost Art of Listening*, "The importance of listening cannot be overestimated." Nichols encourages people to be "reflective listeners." This requires being open, more receptive, and flexible in paying attention to conversations. The value of being a good listener is that you will earn respect from those around you.

The active mental process of listening is also explained by Paul Timm and Sherron Bienvenu in *Straight Talk*. They point out that you should refrain from speaking when gathering information; this is known as supportive listening. When you engage the speaker by concentrating on what he or she is saying, the speaker is more likely to keep speaking to you. If you act distracted, the speaker may terminate the conversation. Being a good listener means that you are actively trying

Active listening is the process of becoming engaged in what the speaker is saying and digesting the information. It is helpful to take notes and ask questions of the speaker.

to retain the information that is being presented to you. Try to think of follow-up questions that you can ask the speaker when he or she finishes speaking on a topic. This will demonstrate to the speaker that you have been listening to what he or she is saying and that you would like additional information.

Remember that listening requires that the listener be alert and focused and make eye contact with the speaker. Resist the urge to debate the speaker, but use the opportunity to respond to the speaker in a manner that conveys that you have been paying attention.

Do's and Don'ts of Networking

• Be confident, but not overly self-assured or arrogant.
• Be friendly to new acquaintances without appearing too anxious or obtrusive.
• Know your strengths and be able to articulate them.
• Be patient—building a successful network of contacts takes time.
• Be creative—explore new ways to connect with others through groups and online.

- Get to the point—don't waste other people's time.
- Don't get too personal in professional settings—keep your personal life to yourself.
- Don't gossip, swear, or sound negative.
- The quality of your contacts is more important than the quantity.
- Offer your help and share your information.

Join In

Starting in school, you are encouraged to join clubs, participate in athletics, and help out in your community. This is your entrance into getting to know your classmates, teachers, and leaders in your neighborhood. These are terrific settings for working on social networking and for setting a foundation for your future networking contacts. Note that it is critical to make connections with people who are older than you, not just

Getting involved in your community will help you build a network of connections. Find out about opportunities in your area to explore your interests and reach your goals.

your peers. This will afford you the opportunity to broaden your community network. Organizations such as the Kiwanis, Lions, and Rotary International are community groups that combine social activities with community service. Joining these organizations is an easy way to connect to your community and increase your social network. Of course, there are local and national nonprofit groups and associations that will teach you to be an advocate for causes you are interested in promoting. Many professionals also volunteer for not-for-profit organizations; this could lead to connecting with people with similar interest and backgrounds. Community service teaches leadership skills and gives you the opportunity to work with all types of people.

Many individuals feel comfortable connecting with new people through sports leagues, religious groups, or political action committees. In these informal settings, you can find many networking opportunities. Remember that any community or social gathering is an opportunity to work on your networking skills. Networking requires action, and just sitting at your computer will not bring you the same results as getting out there and meeting people.

It Takes Effort to Succeed

Experts agree that whether you are preparing for a college interview, a professional meeting, or a job interview, writing your ideas and questions on paper will help you convey your information. Making a list of the points you want to make before you

Everything you choose to do has an impact on your network of contacts. Keep track of your accomplishments and skills so that you can share your uniqueness with others.

call someone or meet in person will keep you from rambling and sounding unprepared. It is also a good idea to practice what you plan to say in front of a friend, teacher, or coworker that you trust to give you good feedback. These techniques will help you find your voice and make networking easier for you.

There is a fine line between making new connections to enhance your career or personal goals and becoming a vulture always looking for something for yourself (like a job or an advantage in a situation). Your network of acquaintances will not make introductions for you if you abuse the relationships that you currently have. Your motives for meeting new people should be to build your relationships, not selfish reasons. Remember that network relationships need to be a two-way street; you need to give before you receive.

As this book points out, there are many resources available to you to become a successful networker. Offering to exchange information with others will strengthen your relationships and shows goodwill. Maybe you can make connections between people in your own social network that could lead to others making a useful connection for you.

Your inner circle of friends, family, and mentors are the people you can always turn to to give you advice, help, and support. When you share your opinions and ideas with new contacts, you bring them in closer to your inner circle. You should always strive to make a good impression on the individuals you meet on a day-to-day basis. You want the buzz about you to always be positive. You are in control of your reputation to the outside world, whether it is in person, at professional or social gatherings, or online when you chat and post with friends.

LinkedIn

LinkedIn is a professional social network that was started in 2003. According to its press center, LinkedIn currently has more than one hundred million people, from more than two hundred countries, registered with the site. This business networking site allows professionals to connect with one another. LinkedIn users set up a profile containing their education, work experience, and expertise. LinkedIn is interesting because when you connect with people on it, their profile pages show the people, companies, and organizations they are already connected to. That opens a world of additional contacts for you. You can follow businesses on their company page by clicking on the link provided on the Web site.

LinkedIn has become a primary source for recruiters to look for candidates to fill a job opening. More than 170 industries have groups on the LinkedIn site. Many Fortune 500 companies have members on LinkedIn. Even nonprofit organizations have joined LinkedIn to find corporations and individuals to provide needed funding for projects. The LinkedIn site has become useful to entrepreneurs and consultants around the world who are interested in increasing their exposure to new opportunities.

How you treat others around you is a reflection of who you are as a person. People will respond to you in a favorable way if you are genuine and sincere. Are you respectful to your parents and siblings in public? Do you treat your coworkers fairly? Do you thank people who do things for you?

Building Lifelong Connections

Building a network of contacts is a lifelong journey that begins when you are young. You will succeed if you constantly open yourself up to new experiences and stay true to your goals. Take advantage of opportunities to grow, such as internships and community service. Sometimes being involved in a hobby or sport can lead to meeting someone who will give you a job or suggest a new path that you should take. You may have to overcome the anxiety of talking face-to-face with a stranger, but if you push yourself to do it, you will find it gets easier with time and practice.

Be prepared for interviews. Dress for success, be an attentive listener, and know how to answer questions about yourself. Do research about the college you are interested in attending or the job that you are interested in securing.

In order to be successful at networking, you must improve your organizational skills. Remember that your success in being an effective networker is directly connected to your ability to be perceived as someone who is honest and hard working. Finding a trusted mentor is valuable in helping you gain perspective on what works for you in honing your networking skills.

Millions of people around the globe are spending more and more time on social networking sites, searching for people and experiences. The connections being made will be lasting if the relationships between the people are real and relevant. If you want to be taken seriously, the information you put out must be beneficial to someone personally or professionally. Real connection comes from turning those online social networking connections into face-to-face interactions.

Networking is most successful when you are helping others first. You will feel a sense of fulfillment when you participate in a meaningful way with your community. You may find that your experience creating new and valuable relationships could actually change your life. Virtual connections cannot replace physical connections between individuals and groups looking to make lasting connections. Life is all about the relationships we make and keep.

You have to be yourself when interacting with others. Do not join clubs, attend meetings, or participate in activities if you are not truly interested in them. You will not be motivated and driven to be good at something if you are doing it only because you think you should or you believe that others want you to do it. If you want to learn to be a leader, you must first be a follower and a student.

This is where your skills at listening and organization will be instrumental. If you are passionate and energetic when you volunteer, perform your job, or prepare for school, the reward will be that others around you will catch your enthusiasm.

The better you are at building strong and lasting personal and professional relationships, the more successful you will be in life. Good communication skills will lead you to accomplishing your goals. Strong relationships are developed over time, and meaningful relationships are worth the time and effort it takes to cultivate them.

GLOSSARY

BLOG An online journal kept by an individual, group, or Web site to record activities or conversations regarding a particular topic.

BODY LANGUAGE Nonverbal communication through the use of facial expressions, posture, and gestures.

CHAT ROOM An Internet forum for communicating with multiple users with common interests, problems, or views.

COMMUNICATION A process by which information is exchanged between individuals through a common system of symbols, signs, or behavior.

DOWNLOAD The process by which information is sent to a computer via the Internet.

FACEBOOK A social networking Web site using customized individual profiles to connect with family and friends.

FEEDBACK Evaluation or information in response to an inquiry.

INSTANT MESSAGING A form of real-time, direct, text-based communication between two or more people.

INTEGRITY The quality of being honest and having strong moral principles.

INTERNET A network linking computers all over the world.

INTERNSHIP A position in which a beginner participates in a program to acquire experience in an occupation, profession, or pursuit.

LINKEDIN A professional network that allows you to be introduced to and collaborate with other professionals.

MENTOR An adviser or trusted counselor who can facilitate an individual's personal or professional growth by sharing knowledge and insight.

MICROBLOGGING Small elements of content sent through Web sites.

MULTIMEDIA Documents that contain audio, graphics, sound, and video elements that can be accessed by the user.

NETWORK A collection of computers interconnected in order to share resources and information.

OBJECTIVE A purpose or goal set to be achieved by a certain time.

PODCAST A combination of iPod and broadcast. It is an audio and visual broadcast that is produced for distribution on the Internet. Professional organizations (such as news media) and amateur producers share their content on the Web.

PROFESSION A job that requires special education, training, or skill.

RELATIONSHIP The way in which two or more people or groups connect together.

SEARCH ENGINE A computer program that finds answers to queries from databases on the Web.

TWITTER A Web site offering an online social networking and microblogging service of text-based messages of up to 140 characters called tweets.

FOR MORE INFORMATION

American Management Academy
1601 Broadway, #7
New York, NY
(212) 586-8100
Web site: http://www.amanet.org
This professional organization provides seminars, workshops, and job
opportunity posts for individuals, corporations, and government
agencies.

Body Language Institute
500 Montgomery Street
Alexandria, VA 22314
(571) 483-2110
Web site: http://www.bodylanguageschool.com
The Body Language Institute is a school that teaches classes and
produces guidebooks to improve body language skills.

Conference Board of Canada
255 Smyth Road
Ottawa, ON K1H 8M7
Canada
(866) 711-2262
Web site: http://www.conferenceboard.ca
This independent not-for-profit research organization in Canada
promotes networking skills and develops leadership techniques.

Forté Foundation
9600 Escarpment, Suite 745 PMB 72
Austin, TX 78749
(512) 535-5157
Web site: http://www.fortefoundation.org

The Forté Foundation is a consortium of major corporations and top business schools committed to educating and directing talented women toward leadership roles in business.

Future Business Leaders of America (FBLA)
1912 Association Drive
Reston, VA 20191-1591
(800) 325-2946
Web site: http://www.fbla.org
FBLA is a nonprofit educational association for students preparing for a career in business.

LeadAmerica
1515 South Federal Highway, Suite 301
Boca Raton, FL 33432
(866) 394-5323
Web site: http://www.lead-america.org
LeadAmerica arranges conferences for middle school and high school students to explore their interests in an interactive learning environment.

National Association of Professional Women (NAPW)
1305 Franklin Avenue, Suite 300
Garden City, NY 11530
(866) 540-6279
Web site: http://www.napw.com
NAPW is an exclusive network for professional women.

National Mentoring Partnership
1680 Duke Street, 2nd Floor
Alexandria, VA 22314

(703) 224-2200

Web site: http://www.mentoring.org

This resource helps people locate mentoring programs that serve
their community.

Small Business Community Network (SBCN)

133 Weber Street N., Suite #3-183

Waterloo, ON N2J 3G9

Canada

(800) 737 5812

Web site: http://www.sbcncanada.org

This Canadian organization gives small businesses networking
opportunities.

Youth Mentoring Connection

1818 S. Western Avenue, Suite 505

Los Angeles, CA 90006

(323) 731-8080

Web site: http://www.youthmentoring.org

This organization supports relationships between adults and youth
and supports school and work mentoring programs.

Web Sites

Due to the changing nature of Internet links, Rosen Publishing has
developed an online list of Web sites related to the subject of this
book. This site is updated regularly. Please use this link to access
the list:

http://www.rosenlinks.com/cwc/procon

FOR FURTHER READING

Auletta, Ken, *Googled*. New York, NY: Penguin Group, 2010.

Baber, Anne, and Lynne Waymon. *Make Your Contacts Count: Networking Know-How for Business and Career Success*. New York, NY: AMACON, 2007.

Fisher, Donna. *Professional Networking for Dummies*. New York, NY: Hungry Minds, 2001.

Jackson, Maggie. *Distracted: The Erosion of Attention and the Coming Dark Age.* Amherst, NY: Prometheus Books, 2008.

Kirkpatrick, David. *The Facebook Effect*. New York, NY: Simon & Schuster, 2011.

Marinez Aleman, Ana M., and Katherine Lynk Wartman. *Online Social Networking on Campus: Understanding What Matters in Student Culture*. New York, NY: Routledge: 2009.

Misner, Ivan, David Alexander, and Brian Hilliard. *Networking Like a Pro: Turning Contacts into Connections*. Irvine, CA: Entrepreneur Press, 2010.

O'Reilly, Tim, and Sarah Milstein. *The Twitter Book*. Sebastopol, CA: O'Reilly Media, 2009.

Prince, Dennis L. *Get Rich with Twitter*. New York, NY: McGraw-Hill, 2010.

Solomon, Muriel. *"What Do I Say When…": A Guidebook for Getting Your Way with People on the Job*. Englewood Cliffs, NJ: Prentice Hall, 1988.

Vermeiren, Jan. *Let's Connect: A Practical Guide for Highly Effective Professional Networking*. Garden City, NY: Morgan James, 2008.

Zack, Devora. *Networking for People Who Hate Networking*. San Francisco, CA: Berrett-Koehler Publishers, 2010.

BIBLIOGRAPHY

Bolles, Richard N. *What Color Is Your Parachute? A Practical Manual for Job-Hunters and Career-Changers*. New York, NY: Crown Publishing Group, 2011.

Crompton, Diane, and Ellen Sautter. *Find a Job Through Social Networking.* 2nd ed. Indianapolis, IN: JIST Works, 2011.

Davidow, William H. *OVERconnected: The Promise and Threat of the Internet*. Harrison, NY: Delphinium Books, 2011.

De Back, Alan. *Get Hired in a Tough Market: Insider Secrets to Find and Land the Job You Need Now*. New York, NY: McGraw-Hill, 2010.

Driver, Janine, and Mariska van Aalst. *You Say More Than You Think: The 7-Day Plan for Using the New Body Language to Get What You Want*. New York, NY: Crown Publishers, 2010.

Greene, Howard R., and Matthew W. Greene. *College Grad Seeks Future: Turning Your Talents, Strengths, and Passions into the Perfect Career*. New York, NY: St. Martin's Griffin Press, 2010.

Hartley, Gregory, and Maryann Karinch. *I Can Read You Like a Book.* Franklin Lakes, NJ: Career Press, 2007.

Merrill, Douglas C., and James A. Martin. *Getting Organized in the Google Era*. New York, NY: Broadway Books, 2010.

Nichols, Michael P. *The Lost Art of Listening*. New York, NY: The Guilford Press, 1995.

Reiman, Tonya. *The Yes Factor: Get What You Want. Say What You Mean. The Power of Persuasive Communication.* New York, NY: Hudson Street Press, 2010.

Spaulding, Tommy. *It's Not Just Who You Know*. New York, NY: Broadway Books, 2010.

Timm, Paul R., and Sherron Bienvenu. *Straight Talk: Written Communication for Career Success.* New York, NY: Routledge, 2011.

INDEX

A

advertising, 24, 54
AOL, 48
attention, paying, 13, 15, 18, 27
audience, knowing your, 20–21

B

background checks, 43
Berman, Thomas, 14
Bienvenu, Sherron, 57
blogs, 15, 24, 42, 48
body language, 9–11, 18, 28, 40
Body Language Institute, 11
business cards, 19

C

chat rooms, 15, 48–50
celebrities, 32, 37
Clementi, Tyler, 54
community service, 24, 26, 60–62, 66
contacts, finding your, 7–15
conventions, 20, 27, 53
Crompton, Dianne, 41, 43
cyberbullying, 53, 54

D

Denham, Tom, 56
Distracted, 24
Dorsey, Jack, 32
Driver, Janine, 11

E

e-mail, 14, 19, 24, 32, 44, 46–47, 50, 53

etiquette, online, 39, 41–50
eye contact, 11, 13, 59

F

Facebook, 6, 14, 15, 31, 32, 33, 35, 37, 39, 46, 51, 54–55
feedback, getting, 9, 22, 64
Find a Job Through Social Networking, 41
Fortune 500 companies, 65

G

Google, 43, 48
Guare, John, 14
guidance counselor, 10 great questions to ask a, 40

H

handshake, how to give a, 11

I

identity theft, 40, 53
information, selling of, 54–55
instant messaging, 32, 50
internships, 18, 22, 25–26, 40, 66
interviews, 15, 18, 20, 40, 62

J

Jackson, Maggie, 24

K

Kiwanis, 62

About the Author

Suzanne Weinick graduated from the University at Albany, State University of New York, in 1986 with a BA in political science and minor in communications. Weinick went on to Hofstra University School of Law and practiced corporate law full-time until she became a mom. She now enjoys writing books for young people.

Photo Credits

Cover (foreground, background), back cover, pp. 4–5, 25, 42–43, 45, 70, 72, 74, 76 Shutterstock; interior graphics © www.istockphoto.com/hypergon; p. 5 © Jeff Greenberg/The Image Works; p. 8 George Boyle/Stockbyte/Getty Images; p. 10 Pinnacle Pictures/Photodisc/Shutterstock; pp. 12–13, 63 Hemera/Thinkstock; p. 17 Peter Dazeley/Digital Vision/Getty Images; pp. 20–21 George Doyle/Stockbyte/Thinkstock; pp. 22–23 © Jim West/The Image Works; p. 30 Bloomberg/Bloomberg via Getty Images; pp. 34, 38 © AP Images; p. 36 © www.istockphoto.com/franckreporter; p. 47 © www.istock-photo.com/Giorgio Fochesato; p. 49 © www.istockphoto.com/YinYang; p. 52 Peter Cade/Iconica/Getty Images; pp. 58–59 BananaStock/Thinkstock; pp. 60–61 Bill Clark/CQ-Roll Call Group/Roll Call/Getty Images; pp. 66–67 Digital Vision/Thinkstock.

Designer: Nicole Russo; Editor: Nicholas Croce;
Photo Researcher: Marty Levick